Mum,

Remember the meek will
inherit the Earth.

Happy Birthday 1983

Lots of love

Liz

xxx
xx
x

GW00569948

# BYGONE HORSHAM

# BYGONE HORSHAM

## Anthony Windrum
### and
## Annabelle Hughes

# PHILLIMORE

1982

Published by
PHILLIMORE & CO. LTD.
London and Chichester

*Head Office*: Shopwyke Hall,
Chichester, Sussex, England

ISBN 0 85033 471 3

Printed and bound in Great Britain by
BILLINGS BOOK PLAN
Worcester

# LIST OF ILLUSTRATIONS

**Carfax**
1. No. 36 on the inner island, last remaining remnant of a medieval building, 1879
2. As above, c.1881
3. Glaysher's, a medieval shop
4. Opposite side of Glaysher's, Middle Street
5. The corner of West Street
6. Dendy's
7. Lintott's grocery wholesalers
8. No. 13 London Road, built c.1830
9. L. C. Pierre's shop, c.1907
10. Pierre's shop, 1908
11. Site of old county gaol, c.1930
12. Site of the brewery, now the Post Office, c.1850
13. The same, about thirty years later
14. The Post Office, about 1900
15. East side of Carfax, c.1900
16. 18th-century buildings on Carfax, c.1965
17. Carfax, c.1912
18. 20th-century architecture
19. East side of inner island, c.1850
20. Looking south, c.1900
21. Looking north, c.1900
22. No. 30, taken in 1881
23. Delivery to the *Stout House*, 1930s
24. Drinking fountain, erected for the Diamond Jubilee, 1897
26. First Town Band, 1864
27. Town Band on 9 August 1902
28. Horsham Recreation Band, 1901
29. Last Town Crier
30. Postmen with pentacycles

**Market Square**
31. Corner of East Street and Market Square, before 1890
32. East side of Market Square, between 1890 and 1899
33. View from the top of the Town Hall, after 1899
34. The old Town Hall, 1912
35. Print of the Town Hall, c.1860
36. Market Square with Town Hall, early 1900s

37. Talbot Court or Lane, now Pump Alley
38. The Town Hall, decorated for the coronation, 1902
39. Frescoes, discovered in the 1930s
40. An Attwater advertisement
41. The Town Hall, used on an advertisement

**The Causeway**
42. Sir Timothy Shelley, M.P., 1790-92
43. Henry Padwick sr.
44. Miss Louisa Churchman
45. Premises of Hunt Brothers, 1906
46. Henry Padwick jr.
47. Looking up Causeway, winter 1908
48. Looking south towards the church
49. Causeway House
50. Causeway, looking north, late 19th-cen.
51. 'Flagstones', late 1880s
52. Children playing in the garden of Causeway Lodge
53. Oldest Free School building, c.1840
54. Almshouses in Normandy
55. Women's side
56. Normandy, showing the almshouses
57. Denne Road and railway bridge, late 19th-century
58. Old town mill and cottages, pre 1868
59. Knifegrinder in Normandy
60. Rear of priest's house (1855)
61. H. Padwick, 1862

**Worthing Road**
62. Site of the brewery, now Tesco
63. Widening Tan Bridge, 1924
64. Free Christian (Unitarian) church
65. Worthing Road seen from Picts Hill, 1904
66. Cricket Field, off the Worthing Road
67. Street scene, 1908
68. Cattle market in 1904
69. Cattle market in the railway yard
70. Henry Burstow
71. Old cottages near the *Green Dragon*

**Springfield Road**
72. General view, c.1900
73. Original Congregational chapel

74. New Congregational chapel
75. Original meeting place of Congregational Church
76. Albion Terrace, west into Springfield Road
77. The Allen brothers' malt store
78. Corner of London Road
79. North Parade before it was widened
80. Bicycle manufacture

**West Street**
81. The *Black Horse* Hotel, *c.*1898
82. Traffic system in the 1950s
83. Cramp's, 1878
84. Cramp's about 20 years later
85. No. 5, still a chemist shop
86. A circus comes to town
87. No. 14, a shoe shop until the 1970s
88. A billhead
89. Saddle and harness makers, William Albery
90. Collection of horse bits in museum
91. The *Castle* Inn
92. Looking east
93. Corner of West Street and Carfax
94. After the fire at No. 63
95. The Hunt brothers' business

**London Road**
96. Wickersham's Forge
97. Wickersham Lane
98. Present entrance to Medwin Walk
99. The Methodist church
100. Sussex Place
101. Oldest remaining building on north side
102. No. 32, once an inn
103. Mr Mills' cottages
104. Major Middleton
105. Ockendens, No. 18
106. Corner of Carfax and London Road, where was once the *Lamb* Inn

**North Street**
107. Looking south to town centre, pre-1914
108. Padwick's house, later Stedman's
109. Present Sun Alliance premises
110. Aerial view from St Mark's steeple

111. Perry Place
112. St Mark's in the 1840s
113. Chart's store
114. Turner's shop, pre 1914
115. Linden Terrace
116. Old Mr Voice
117. Park House
118. Rear of Park House, 1860s
119. Robert Henry Hurst, jnr., M.P.
120. Original station building
121. The *Station* Hotel, early 1900s
122. North Chapel
123. Collyer's School, *c.*1893
124. The Cottage Hospital
125. Park Nurseries
126. Trade Bill heading

**East Street**
127. Looking east from Carfax, *c.*1900
128. No. 23, part of medieval hall-house
129. Junction with Park Street, looking west, *c.*1900
130. Allman's Nurseries
131. Present-day buildings at Allman's Corner
132. Looking east towards the Iron Bridge, early 20th century
133. Demolishing air-raid shelters on same site
134. Train accident near Iron Bridge
135. 'Bishop's', at the junction with Denne Road
136. Looking towards Carfax, *c.*1900
137. Closer view of 30 East Street
138. Decorating firm at No. 18

**Miscellaneous**
139. Sketch of Fred Bridges
140. Alfred Shrubb
141. Only photograph of Horsham windmills
142. Carnival float, *c.*1900
143. Tradesmen's cricket match, 1899
144. Costermonger, 1950s
145. Committee of Horsham Mutual Improvement Society, *c.*1891
146. Bill heading for Lintott & Son
147. Horsham postmen, after World War One
148. 2nd Volunteer Battalion, Royal Sussex Regiment, 1900s

## ACKNOWLEDGEMENTS

The authors are indebted to the following for the loan of pictures: Miss K. Bates, Mr G. Coomber, Mr C. Cramp, Mr H. Glaysher, Mr and Mrs. R. Griffiths, Horsham Museum Society, Miss B. Hurst, Mr G. Jackson, Mr R. Luff, Mr G. Moulding, Mrs Robbé, Mr M. Shirley, Mr A. Wailes. We are also grateful to those who lent pictures for which there was no space.

# CARFAX

The origin of this name is not certainly known. Traditionally it has been interpreted as the meeting of four ways (a corruption of 'quatre vois') but before the 18th century the spellings were variations on 'Scarfolkes'. It has been suggested that this meant 'scarce of people', i.e. a waste area, which could be used for an open market place.

Certainly from ancient times fairs and markets were held at Carfax, and evidence for its 'open' nature is suggested by the fact that no burgages existed in the central area. As today, it has always been the heart of the town. Tudor and earlier buildings still exist on the east and south sides, but redevelopment of the other two sides has swept away anything earlier than the early 19th-century.

Until Horsham was forced to take notice of the appalling sanitary conditions which prevailed in the late-19th century, Carfax was the scene of itinerants' encampments connected with the fairs, and there were many presentments to the courts about depositing filth and blocking gutters.

The county gaol was on the north side until 1779, and nearby on the centre island were the stocks, pillory and bull ring. Behind the present Richmond Terrace was a brewery and hop-garden.

1.  The only remaining remnant of a medieval building now on the inner island is No. 36. This drawing by Charles Burstow (1879) gives some idea of the adjacent structure which would have been similar and may even have been part of the same building.

2. (*above*) This is the same building as in plate 1, taken
*c.*1881, when Clark's was a 'curing house and ice stores'.

3. (*left*) Opposite was Glaysher's, discovered in the 196[
to have been a medieval shop, which after being dismantl[
is to be re-erected at Singleton Open Air Museum.

4. (*below*) The other side of Glaysher's in Middle Stree[
also the family jewellery shop.

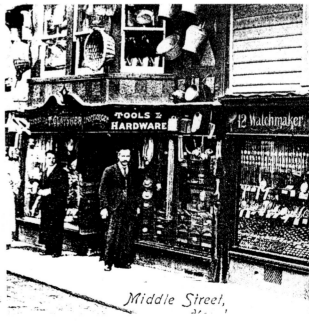

On the corner of West Street, a draper's business has existed for over a century. No. 8 is now Chart & Lawrence,
re shown as Duke's in 1898.

6. Opposite the western corner of Carfax and Middle Street stood
Dendy's, a famous family name in non-conformist Horsham. The
building was demolished in the 1960s.

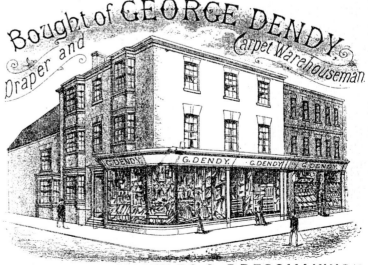

7. Lintott's was a successful grocery wholesalers on the site of the present Sterling Buildings. The family house is on the right. All were demolished after the last war.

8. A typical professional man's house built *c.*1830, with Ionic pilasters similar to those in Brunswick Place in London Road. This was No. 13, demolished in the early 1970s.

9.  On the inner island, opposite Lintott's, was L. C. Pierre's shop at No. 44. This picture dates from *c.*1907.

10.  Pierre's shop is also in this photograph of 1908 showing the trees on Gaol Green where the stocks and whipping post stood.

11.  Opposite this site was the old county gaol from 1600 to 1779. Nothing remains except the gaoler's house on the corner with North Street, covered over with later walls and roof. This picture was taken *c.*1930.

12.   This panorama was sketched by Thomas Mann *c.*1850 and shows the site of the brewery where the Post Office now stands. Behind, there was a hop-garden.

14.   The Post Office at the beginning of the 20th century, demolished 1972.

The same row of buildings as in plate 12, about thirty years later.

BAND STAND & POST OFFICE HORSHAM

15. The east side of the Carfax still has some old buildings, shown in the centre of this picture taken *c.*1900. Note the Jubilee Fountain in use, and the bandstand which had just been erected.

16. In the 18th century sites on Carfax were sold by the Duke of Norfolk (who did not own them) and permanent buildings were erected. This picture dates from *c.*1965.

7. The motor age is beginning to make its impact. Here, c.1912, is a view looking into the Carfax from Market Square. The *King's Head* has been an inn for centuries and was also the office of the Inland Revenue from 1855 to 1881, hence the sign on the wall.

8. Austere 20th-century architecture is replacing earlier styles.

19. Another drawing by Thomas Mann of the east side of the inner island c. 1850. On the right is now a bank, on the left a shoe shop containing part of the original building (see plate 1).

20. Looking south from the north-east corner c. 1900.

21. A view looking north c.1900.

22.   This is No. 30 in 1881 where the Horsham Building Society now stands. The Richardson family had been plumbers in Horsham since the 18th century.

23.   The Horsham Brewery making a delivery to the *Stout House* in the 1930s when lorries could still have solid tyres.

24. The Carfax has always been ideal for large public celebrations such as coronations and jubilees; this is probably Queen Victoria's Diamond Jubilee in 1897.

25. The 1897 Jubilee was marked by the erection of a drinking fountain. The official photograph shows (*left to right*) Jury Cramp, A. M. Coleman, William Hull, H. P. Thorpe (?), J. Hicks, Rev. Bell (?), E. J. Perry, Arthur Aldridge, Robert Henry Hurst Jr., who performed the ceremony. To the right of the fountain, Rev. A. F. Young, Alfred Agate, Canon Evan Daniel, C. J. Stott, E. I. Bostock, John Marsh (?), Samuel Mitchell, Thomas Richardson, Dr. F. W. Kinneir, William Lintott.

26.  Horsham has always been proud of its bands. The first Town Band of 1864 is shown here. Back row (*left to right*), H. Mills, F. Feist, I. Rogers, H. Mills Jr.; middle row, P. Knight, R. Humphrey, D. Wood, C. Mills; front row, C. Attwater, O. Snelling, M. Etheridge, H. Leggatt.

27. The Town Band on 9 August 1902 at the festivities for the Coronation of King Edward VII. At the back, C. Shoubridge and H.Jupp; middle row, C. Barker, Allen Etheridge, Robert Etheridge, W. Etheridge, G. Etheridge, Henry Harris; front row C. Smallwood, H. C. Attwater, C. Scott, William Harris (Bandmaster), H. Baker, C. Rogers, G. Burstow. Seated, G. Scrase and Jack Boxall.

28. There have been other bands and this one was known as the Horsham Recreation Band in 1901. William Albery (centre) was the conductor.

Town criers were often heard in the Carfax and the last one, William Law, won ational competition in 1912.

30.  There have been many post offices in and around the Carfax, and many modes of transport have been used by the postmen. These pentacycles were most unwieldy and did not last long.

# MARKET SQUARE

This is the only remaining street name that reminds the visitor of the market which was the reason for Horsham's burgeoning success in the medieval period, and which occupied the whole site bounded by the top of the Causeway and the west, north and east sides of the modern Carfax. From earliest times, this corner almost certainly contained the market house—the administrative building for the market, fairs and borough business. Originally, this was probably a timber-framed building on arches over a covered market area, which later offered facilities for the Assizes, held in Horsham from 1306 until the early-19th century. The building was replaced at least twice, each time by a more substantial construction.

In the mid-18th century, one of the Hurst family, Richard, was a mercer who lived and kept a shop in Market Square. His eldest daughter, Sarah, maintained a love affair with Henry Smith of the Marines, whose mother lived in Chantry House in the Causeway, for 10 years, much of the time unknown to family and friends, until they were married secretly at Slinfold Parish church in 1762.

1. The corner of East Street and Market Square at which W. Loxley, grocer and provisions merchant, had a business before 1890. By 1903 it was Freeman, Hardy & Willis; now it is a house agents. The drapers next door was Durrant's.

32.   The east side of Market Square between 1890 and 1899 when the new *Anchor* Hotel was built. This picture
shows Durrant's, the drapers, the old *Anchor* Hotel and the entrance to the hotel yard. Roberts, furniture and
upholsterers and Ashford, chemists, were the next properties on the right.

33. A view from the top of the Town Hall, post-1899, showing the new *Anchor* Hotel and a coach calling at the *Kings Head*.

34. A Thomas Mann drawing (1912) of the old Town Hall, probably built for the town by the Eversfields of Denne. Before the 1812 rebuilding it had an open market beneath. It bears some resemblance to a drawing on a map of 1770, and may be earlier.

*Rock & Co London, N° 3806.*　　　　　　　　　*27 Aug.st 1860*

*Town Hall Horsham, Sussex.*

35. (*opposite*) Print of the Town Hall, *c.* 1860.

36. An early-20th-century picture of Market Square showing the Town Hall, Tanner & Chart (where Grants now is), the 1899 *Anchor* Hotel, and (Cramp's) *Temperance* Hotel, once at No. 10. The *Talbot* Inn sign is also visible (north side of Pump Alley and Talbot Court).

37. Talbot Court or Lane, now Pump Alley, showing possible medieval timbering on the right. This was the site of a burgage property.

38. The Town Hall decorated for the Coronation of Edward VII. The panels show the royal arms, those of the town and those of the Dukes of Norfolk.

39. In the 1930s these frescoes were discovered in the premises of the Y.M.C.A., now Hoad & Taylors, on the south side of Pump Alley. They are probably late 16th-century wall-decorations. Two and a quarter bays of an earlier building (pre-1550) are at right-angles to the Tudor building which fronts the Market Square. This was another burgage site.

40. An Attwater advertisement.

41. The Town Hall, used as a trademark for Worth & Company's tobaccos.

# THE CAUSEWAY

The word 'causeway' is descriptive in origin, meaning a 'raised footpath' and this is precisely what the Horsham Causeway was from earliest times—a raised footpath linking the Parish Church with the Market Place. In the first document (the 1524 subsidy) that records Horsham streets by name, 'South Street' is used to designate most of the length of the street now called the Causeway. The ecclesiastical boundaries probably extended as far as the present No. 18 on the east side, and perhaps as far as Minstrels on the west. Nearer the Market Place the plots, with or without buildings, were all burgages as is shown on the earliest known plan of the borough which dates from 1611.

In the early medieval period the Causeway would have presented a more open appearance, with fewer and smaller houses, and with plots extending as far as Denne Road on the east, and Worthing Road on the west. These plots would have been managed as smallholdings, many containing orchards, barns, outbuildings, and even, in one case, a horsemill.

There are at least five complete houses still identifiable as medieval, and portions of original medieval properties are contained within three or four more of the present houses. There are references in the 17th-century churchwardens' accounts to poor-houses, to the Dye house in the Normandy at the east end of the church, to a bell house built in the early 1600s and to the school building called Little Horsham. Nineteenth-century photographs and drawings show at least one medieval building.

The house next to Teagstones, which is 200 years older than the date on its gable, has been known as Chantry House since the 18th century and is a reminder of the four chantries that were once established in the Parish church. In 1982 it was discovered that the core of this house is a medieval barn.

Parts of the Causeway are still paved with huge slabs of Horsham stone, used extensively in the area for paving, flooring and roofing. A Horsham 'sclatter' was employed on the roof of the hall of the London Company of Drapers in 1425 and the churchwardens' accounts contain references to loads of stone 'for the Church casey' and payments made for 'healing the Church'. The Michells of Stammerham, now the site of Christ's Hospital, seem to have worked the quarry there, and supplied Horsham stone over a wide area.

42. Sir Timothy Shelley, M.P. 1790-92, father of the poet P. B. Shelley, owned property in the Causeway.

43.  Henry Padwick sr. began life as a money-lender and acquir[ed] the Manor House from Edward Tredcroft (*c.*1860) in settlemen[t] of loans.

44.  Miss Louisa Churchman, eldest daughter of the Churchman grocers, whose premises stood on the corner of South Street and Middle Street in the early 1900s (now Abbey National). She became a J.P. and town councillor and was associated with the W.E.A. A hall named after her used to stand in North Street, south of the ABC cinema.

46. Henry Padwick jr. (1828-1916). One of his brothers, a doctor, lived at 29 North Street in the 1920/30s on the site of the present Sun Alliance offices.

45. The premises of Hunt Brothers in 1906, on the corner of South Street and West Street, now replaced by Lloyds Bank. Churchman Burt's present office can be seen to the left.

47.   Looking north up the Causeway in the winter of 1908.

48.   Looking south towards the church. 'Minstrels', probably another medieval hall-house originally, was then three cottages, part ship-lapped and Randall, a breeches-maker, lived in the northern most part *c*.1881. The bootmakers Voice and Vaughn also lived there between 1880 and 1900.

49. Causeway House when first used as Horsham Museum *c.* 1940-41. A large part of it is almost certainly a medieval hall-house. Note the bay window on the front of No. 8, now gone.

50. A view of the Causeway, looking north, in the late-19th century, showing the east side from Nos. 19 and 20.

51. 'Flagstones' in the late-1880s with Mr. Cork and Jury Cramp (of the *Temperance* Hotel, and West Street clockmaker) standing in the foreground.

Sketch of children playing in the garden
Causeway Lodge—a Hurst home.

53. A sketch of the oldest Free School building (the Collyers foundation) in about 1840 by Augusta Hurst. Called Little Horsham in the 17th century, St. Mary's Primary School now occupies the site.

54. The almshouses in the Normandy before the 20th-century rebuilding. This picture shows the gateway leading to the Normandy.

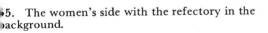

55. The women's side with the refectory in the background.

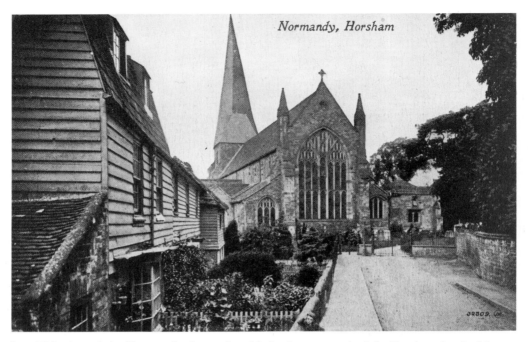

*Normandy, Horsham*

56.  This view of the Normandy shows the old almshouses on the left. Horsham has had 'poor-houses' on this site since 1447. The present building was erected in 1844.

57.  Late 19th-century view of the bottom of Denne Road and the railway bridge over Cobbetts Bridge.

*Denne Road, Horsham*

58. A view of the old Town Mill (pre-1868) with cottages. One cottage remained when the present Mill was built and it was not demolished until the 1930s. Prewetts worked this Mill during the late 19th century. Most of this building was enclosed within the present 19th-century construction.

59. A knifegrinder in Normandy, after the demolition of the old priest's house, but before the rebuilding of the almshouses.

60.  Drawing of the rear of the priest's house (1885) once in the Normandy at the end of the churchyard.

61. A photograph by H. Padwick (1862) of the parish church from the south, before the *Teulon* restoration of 1865.

# WORTHING ROAD

The ancient way to the south ran down Denne Road and over Denne Hill, but the present Worthing Road was made out of a country lane in order to avoid the Denne Estate altogether. It was turnpiked in 1764.

62. The site of the brewery is now occupied by Tesco. Here the visit of Edward VII in 1905 is being celebrated.

63. Increasing traffic meant the rebuilding and widening of Tan Bridge in 1924. A bridge over the Arun at this point has existed since at least the early 17th century.

64. In 1720 the Free Christian (now Unitarian) church was built, and its Minister in 1893, the Rev. J. J. Marten, founded the Museum Society. The church was particularly active in cultural matters.

65.    Seen from Pict's Hill, the Worthing Road near the *Fox and Hounds* Inn (now the *Boar's Head* Tavern) in 1904. Pict's Hill was difficult for horse traffic to climb and was lowered in 1809. Before the road was turnpiked in 1764 the main road south from Horsham was through Denne Park.

66.    The cricket field just off the Worthing Road used to be the barrack field at the time of the Napoleonic Wars, but it was given to the town in 1850. It has been a famous county ground, said to have the finest setting in England. Here the Chamber of Trade team in 1913 is pictured during a match against the West Sussex Constabulary. From the back (*left to right*) H. C. Hunt, A. Bryce, H. C. Attwater, R. C. Agate, P. T. Martin, A. T. Albery, J. Grounds, S. Hunt, J. H. Knapman, T. L. Lane, W. F. Sendall, Umpire A. Oakes.

# BISHOPRIC

Originally 'Archbishopric', the name derives from lands owned by the manor of Tarring-cum-Marlpost whose seigneur was the Archbishop of Canterbury. Always a wide street, it was the site of the cattle and sheep market after they had been evicted from the Carfax in the last century. At market times it was said that almost every cottage was a beer-house to serve the market population.

67.   Street scene in 1908, etching by Bertha Hornung.

68.   After the cattle market had been turned out of the Carfax in 1852, it was held in the Bishopric until 1914. This picture shows the market in 1904.

69. The 20th century is necessarily changing Horsham. The cattle market was invaded by motor traffic and was moved to the railway yard. Note the telephone pole; very few people were yet on the phone.

70. A picture of Henry Burstow, whose *Reminiscences* are a Horsham classic. Born at No. 24 in 1824, he was a bellringer at the Parish church for 60 years. He relates that during his childhood many of the cottagers in the Bishopric made clay pipes.

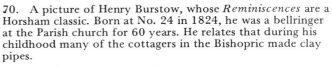

71. Some of these old cottages like nos. 12-14 next to the *Green Dragon*, were pulled down in 1931.

# SPRINGFIELD ROAD

From the 'spring field' where a Queen Anne house is to be found, this was the exit road from Horsham to London, and when turnpiked in 1755 contributed important revenues to Horsham and aided its development.

72.  A general view, *c.*1900, showing the Roman Catholic chapel on the right, with the Congregational chapel behind.

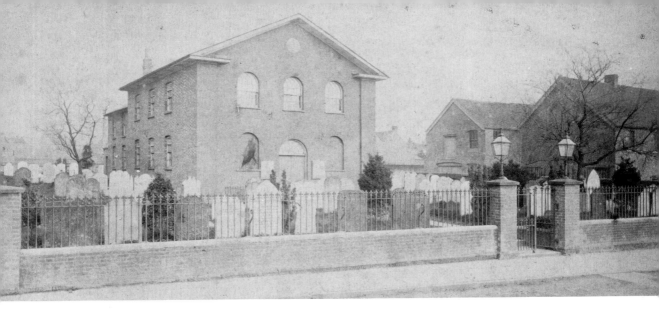

73.   The original Congregational chapel was built in 1816 on the Swan Meadow.

74.   In 1873 a larger building, pictured here, was erected. This was replaced in 1982 by an office block incorporating a chapel.

75.  Before the chapel was built the congregation met, from 1800, in this house on the site of the present *Michell Arms*.

76. Albion Terrace looking west into Springfield Road. The houses are early Victorian.

77. The famous malt stores where the Allen brothers defrauded the Excise for 10 years by hiding undisclosed stocks of malt behind false walls.

78. At the corner with London Road, the Royal British School was built in 1814. Jackson's Garage took over the premises in the early 1900s. From left to right; Lucas, Boorer, D. King, G. Russell, G. Jackson, G. Garner, J. Grayett, J. Chriss (later captain of the Fire Brigade), Bob Ireland, E. Rule, E. Humphrey, W. Gravett, H. Ireland, Ned Fuller, E. Jackson, C. Rogers.

79. A view of North Parade before it was widened, looking towards Springfield Road in the 1900s.

80.  Bicycles were also made locally. Here are some more Jackson employees. Left to right; front row: Bill Gent,
Bob Ireland, H. Jackson, G. Jackson, Edwin Knight, A. Gordon. Back row: G. Urrey, C. Rogers, D. King, J. Jackson,
G. Lucas, Jim Chriss.

# WEST STREET

Although West Street has been a main shopping area for centuries it never contained any burgages. Today no buildings dated earlier than the 18th century still exist. As in many towns, one can trace generations of the same family fulfilling the same occupations, though nowadays, due to the invasion of the multinationals, only one or two such families still remain. Until the early years of the 20th century there were several public houses which thrived with business from the Cornmarket, which has since gone, although parts of the building remain.

81. Looking east *c.*1898. The *Black Horse* Hotel was demolished in the 1960s to allow for shop development. The premises on the opposite corner (No. 35, Stephens, ironmongers) also disappeared at this time and is now a vacant site.

82. By the 1950s, a one-way system was introduced in West Street towards the Carfax.

83.  Cramp's in 1878. The business was founded in 1872 by Jury Cramp (in doorway). In the group, left to right: Mr Weller, William Anderson, Mr Masters. Upstairs, Alfred J. Cramp and his sister May.

84.  Cramp's about twenty years later, when enlarging the premises meant removal of the small Office shown in No. 83. The next two buildings to the right are now gone.

85.   No. 5 is still a chemist shop. Brassington's was here from 1896 to 1915.

86.   Until the end of the First World War, the streets of Horsham could easily be
used for processions without dislocation of traffic. Here a circus has come to town.

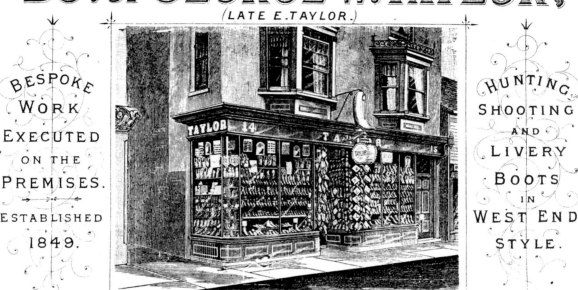

THE GOLDEN BOOT,
HORSHAM,

189

Mr

## BOT. OF GEORGE W. TAYLOR,
### (LATE E. TAYLOR.)

BESPOKE
WORK
EXECUTED
ON THE
PREMISES.

ESTABLISHED
1849.

HUNTING,
SHOOTING
AND
LIVERY
BOOTS
IN
WEST END
STYLE.

INTEREST CHARGED ON OVERDUE ACCOUNTS.

87.  No. 14 was a shoe shop for many years until the 1970s. Due to the tanneries in the town, much footwear was made locally.

88.  A lot of artistry went into the design of billheads when paper and printing were cheap. Public houses were used for bargaining over the price of corn until the Corn Exchange was built in 1866. It can still be seen at No. 29.

THE BLACK HORSE COMMERCIAL INN,
and Market House,

WEST STREET,

HORSHAM.

JAS. CLARKE, PROPRIETOR,

Wholesale Wine & Spirit Merchant.

Families supplied.   Horses for Hire.

SHEATHER & CO.
LONDON.

89. (*right*) The famed local historian William Albery spent all his working hours in the saddle and harness business at No. 49, started by his family in 1810.

90. (*below*) Albery gave his magnificent collection of horse bits to the Museum before he died in 1952.

91. The *Castle* Inn at No. 56 on the north side of West Street disappeared in 1908.

92. A view looking east. Cheeseman's Piano Warehouse at No. 53 faces the Corn Exchange at No. 29.

Adjacent to Rice's is Chart &
Lawrence, Milliners and General Draper's,
the corner of West Street and Carfax.

94.   After the fire at No. 63. The Rice family came to Horsham in 1895 and took over Tuffin's harness-makers', but soon made cycle manufacture their chief activity.

95.   Hunt Brothers at Nos. 1 and 2. Their business remained on the site until 1967, but this photograph was taken before the fire at Rice's (opposite, No. 63) in 1909.

# LONDON ROAD

London Road was originally a track from the Skarfolkes (modern Carfax) which led to the Borough Pound, sited roughly where Clement Clarke's office building now stands. The Pound was the place where lost and straying animals were kept until claimed by their rightful owners. It also led to Beane Bridge, and eventually became known as London Road, as it led from the Carfax to London via Dorking. One of the tolls was sited near its northernmost junction with North Parade.

Early maps and records suggest that settlement along this track was mainly in the form of 'crofts' or smallholdings, which ran back into the area that is now the Park, and that there were some of the original burgage plots. By the 18th century it had become more of a road than a track and houses and cottages fronted onto the road. The Park swallowed up much of the croft land and gradually the network of roads— Wickersham Road, Madeira Avenue and Linden Terrace—emerged which are now largely covered over by Albion Way.

96. Wickersham's Forge stood roughly where the Park Surgery is now, and the name is still over a business on the Carfax.

97. Wickersham Lane.

Established 1842.

*D. Wickersham, R.S.S.,*

Shoeing & Jobbing Forges,

3, WICKERSHAM'S LANE,

*Horsham.*

Horses carefully Measured and Shod.

98.   At the point where London Road used to leave the Carfax, now the
entrance to Medwin  Walk, on the left, stood 'Bornes', one of the oldest
remaining burgage houses dating from c. 1400, with additions built in the
16th and 17th centuries. Both this, and the late-18th to 19th-century
building next to it (which housed Cotchings, the solicitors) were demolished to make way for the development of the central area in the 1970s.
Cotchings incorporated the firm of Thomas Medwin, whose papers are
among the Museum archives.

99.   The Methodist church, which
was built in 1832. Brunswick Place
carried its date (1835) above an
imposing porch and was at one
time the home of the widow of
Thomas Stedman of Bewbush
Manor.

100.   Sussex Place is clearly Horsham's contribution to the Regency period.
From the plan of Horsham in Albery's book showing the various gaol sites,
the House of Correction stood somewhere on this site until 1779. In 1731 the
then Master, William Ede, fitted up a room in his own house in London Road
as the 'house of correction' and this was later described in less than glowing
terms by John Howard (1773) though by then it was being run by a widow
whose husband had died of gaol fever.

101. The oldest remaining building on the north side of London Road is possibly No. 46, as is strongly suggested by the level of foundations compared with the present road surface. A recent renovation also revealed a tile dated 1752.

102. No. 32 was at one time an inn called the *Good Intent*, and was next to Thorn's Electric Printing Works.

103. Mr Mills' cottages—a baker in 1882— stood where a modern brick block is now, and Hedgers was still operating in the 1930s.

104. Major Middleton, one of the men instrumental in the building of the Capitol as the Blue Flash Cinema, once lived in the Old House.

105. In 1937 William Albery, Horsham's antiquarian, was living in No. 18, which he called Ockendens, after the burgage site on which it stood.

106. King & Chasemore's building has long been prominent on the corner of the Carfax, where it once ran into London Road, although in 1770 it was known as the *Lamb* Inn.

# NORTH STREET/HURST ROAD

This street led out from the Carfax towards Rough Heath (now Roffey) between Horsham and Crawley, and on to Rusper. From the 13th century the town had held close links with the Priory at Rusper, which had been granted part of the parish church tithes. A farmhouse called Cockmans, remains of which may be those discovered during renovation work in Park House, marked the northernmost point of the borough, and the present Park, not created until the 18th century, consisted of agricultural holdings and crofts.

On the 1841 Tithe Map, large parts of the area to the east of North Street were still marked as fields, meads, or nursery gardens. Even in the early-20th century the road still presented a very rural aspect and it was only the development of rail links and the electrification of the line that quickly transformed North Street because it was the route between the station and the town centre.

The line of Hurst Road, which now marks the northernmost boundary of Horsham Park, joining North Street to North Parade, was no more than a series of access tracks to the farms that were dotted around this area until the end of the last century—Angus Farm, Lambsbottom Farm, Nightingale Farm—most only perpetuated now in street names.

The Hurst family has been part of Horsham's history from medieval times, and Horsham Park was created as an adjunct to their 18th-century family mansion—now in council ownership. In the 1890s Colonel Hurst gave land to the north of his estate for the benefit of the town—for the Cottage Hospital, the first Art School and the re-siting of Collyers Grammar School. The necessary access road was understandably named after him in gratitude and now contains further public buildings, such as the fire station, hospital extension, police station, law courts and the Post Office depot.

107.   Looking south towards the town centre before World War One. On the left is Perry Place, a medieval burgage property, the materials of which were used after 1903/4 in the building of 'Fullers' at Mannings Heath. Mid-centre i a second medieval house, now Cake and Sons. The spire of St Mark's, which was added to the church (1840/41) in 1870 can also be seen. On the right is the *Hurst Arms*, the present newsagent and confectioner, and the cottages tha were on the site of the public library until the 1950s. Just south of the *Hurst Arms* was the house on the Sun Alliance site that once belonged to Dr. Padwick, whose father owned the Manor House.

108.   A view south showing Padwick's house, later Stedman's.

109.   Now the premises of Sun Alliance (cf. modern card of Sun Alliance).

110.   An aerial view from St Mark's Steeple, looking north. Notice the open space on the right before the station.

111. Perry Place, a typical medieval house, with central range and crosswings. It stood on the site south of the ABC cinema.

112. St Mark's in the 1840s without its steeple and later extensions.

113.  Chart's store, now the Model shop next to Cake and Son.

114. Turner's shop, before the First World War. Next to the present library, it is still a newsagent and fancy goods shop.

115. Linden Terrace which ran off North Street almost opposite St Mark's, and was razed when Albion Way was constructed. The corner is still known as the Linden site.

16.  Old Mr Voice outside his house. Voice's Patent Blind and Cornice Pole works was at 19 North Street in 1905, and the Voices have been in Horsham since at least 1524, when the name appeared as 'Foys'.

117.  Park House as it appeared in 1865.

118.  The rear of Park House in the 1860s.

119.  Robert Henry Hurst, jnr., M.P., 1865-75. The Hurst family first appeared in Horsham in the late 14th century and owned or occupied many well-known properties at various times including the Moated House at Chennellsbrook, the present Museum (9 Causeway) and Park House.

120.  The original station building (1848) which was not replaced until the 1930s.

121.  The *Station* Hotel in the early 1900s, which still stands opposite the station virtually unchanged.

*North Chapel, Horsham W.I.*

122.  North Chapel, the left-hand side of which is medieval (pre-1550) with an oriel window and vyse which was built to accommodate a staircase when the open hall was floored in. It is thought to have been connected with the Brotherhood which ran the early poorhouse in the Normandy and a chantry in the parish church.

123. Collyer's School just after it was built in 1893. The school was moved from a site near the parish church.

124. The Cottage Hospital, built by subscription in 1892, upon land given by Col. Hurst.

125. Park Nurseries which stood on the site of the district planning office, opposite Northchapel. Probably similar to the remaining cottages on the corner of North Street and Hurst Road.

126. A trade bill heading. Daniel Richardson who combined taxidermy with his other skills.

# EAST STREET

If the County Archaeologist is right in believing that the Saxon settlement probably originated at the crossroads of East Street, Park Street and Denne Road, then East Street would be an early access to the growing market area of Carfax. The street contains some medieval buildings on the north side, and a splendid medieval house at the corner of Denne Road, formerly called Bishop's. From the crossroads towards the centre of the town, the buildings have always been used for commercial purposes but eastwards there were many residences until this century.

127. Looking east from Carfax, *c.*1900. The *King's Head* was being changed from stables to garage.

128.  There are still some very old houses in East Street. No. 23 is part of a medieval hall-house. This photograph was taken about 1860.

129.  Facing west at the junction with Park Street, c.1900. This may have been the site of the original Saxon settlement.

130. Allman's Nurseries was at this same corner until 1890.

131. The present-day buildings at Allman's Corner under construction, c. 1890.

132. An early-20th century photograph looking east towards the Iron Bridge. The timbered building (No. 50) on the right still exists.

133.  Demolishing air-raid shelters after World War Two, on the same site as caption 132.

134.  (*opposite*) In 1866 two trains collided near the Iron Bridge and this is the impression of a local artist who saw
the crash. Snow had broken the telegraph wires and prevented a warning being given.

Sketch of Collision at Northampton, Eyre & Bridge

135.   A grand medieval burgage at the south-east corner of the junction with Denne Road. Known as 'Bishop's' after the family occupants, much of it remains today as a newsagents and cafe.

136.   Looking towards the Carfax around 1900. The ironmonger's on the left (No. 30) followed a common custom of displaying goods outside.

137.   A closer view of No. 30 East Street with a large gas lantern outside. Electricity did not come to the town until 1901.

138.   A well-known decorating firm at No. 18 (then Nos. 59/60). W. Sendall is wearing the hat with W. Bolwell on his left.

**139.** (*left*) A sketch of Fred Bridges, sometime chairman of the Urban District Council, who kept a fabric shop in the Carfax.

**140.** (*right*) Alfred Shrubb was a phenomenal runner over many distances from one to 11 miles during the first decade of this century. He became the World's Amateur Long Distance Champion.

**141.** Of the four windmills in the Horsham borough, only one photograph is known. This is the Star Mill which stood from ?1777 to 1895 at Roffey. The miller's cottage is still standing.

142.   The tradition of a carnival in Horsham is an old one. Outside the *Bedford* Hotel *c.*1900 this float reflects the Boer War atmosphere.

143.   A tradesmen's cricket match in 1889. There are six or more different styles of headgear.

144.  One of the last of the old costermongers in the early 1950s.

145.  The committee of the Horsham Mutual Improvement Society, *c.*1891. *Left to right*, back row: David Price, John Hicks, James Harrington, Roger Henwood, Henry Carter, S. Mitchell. Middle row: H. R. Carter, Rev. A. F. Young, C. J. Stott, W. H. (Billie) Anderson (Bowler). Fron row: Robert Crowhurst, Charlie Smith.

146. Chinese-style bill heading for Lintott & Son, Grocers of South Street.

147. Horsham postmen pictured just after the First World War.

148.   The 2nd Volunteer Battalion, Royal Sussex Regiment, in the 1900s. Sir Cecil Hurst is seated behind the drum.